Beginning Piano Solo

ENCANTO: Music from the Motion Picture Soundtrack

Disney

ENCANTO

Original Songs by Lin-Manuel Miranda

ISBN 978-1-70516-615-4

Visit Hal Leonard Online at
www.halleonard.com

Contact us:
Hal Leonard
7777 West Bluemound Road
Milwaukee, WI 53213
Email: info@halleonard.com

In Europe, contact:
Hal Leonard Europe Limited
42 Wigmore Street
Marylebone, London, W1U 2RN
Email: info@halleonardeurope.com

In Australia, contact:
Hal Leonard Australia Pty. Ltd.
4 Lentara Court
Cheltenham, Victoria, 3192 Australia
Email: info@halleonard.com.au

CONTENTS

THE FAMILY MADRIGAL

Music and Lyrics by
LIN-MANUEL MIRANDA

With a Latin groove

This is our home, we've got ev - 'ry gen - er - a - tion.

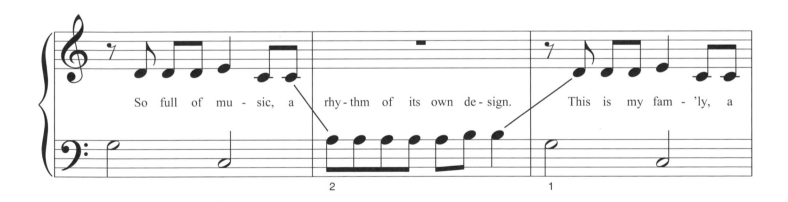

So full of mu - sic, a rhy - thm of its own de - sign. This is my fam - 'ly, a

per - fect con - stel - la - tion. So man - y stars, and ev - 'ry - bod - y gets to shine.

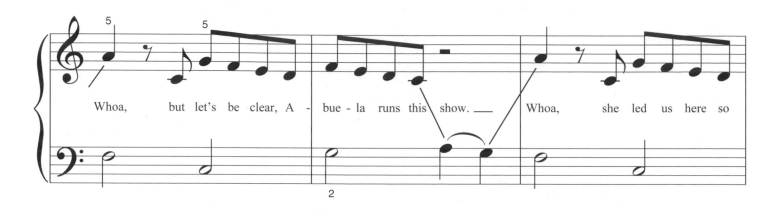

Whoa, but let's be clear, A - bue - la runs this show. ___ Whoa, she led us here so

man - y years a - go. _____ Whoa, and ev - 'ry year our

fam - 'ly bless-ings grow! There's just a lot you've sim - ply got to know, so!

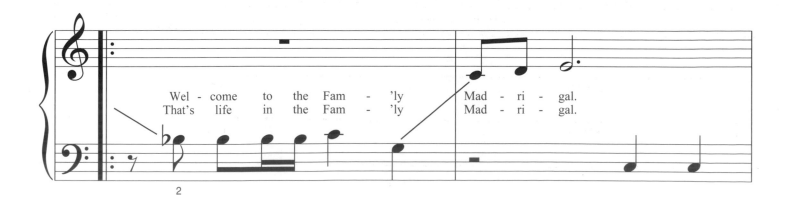

Wel - come to the Fam - 'ly Mad - ri - gal.
That's life in the Fam - 'ly Mad - ri - gal.

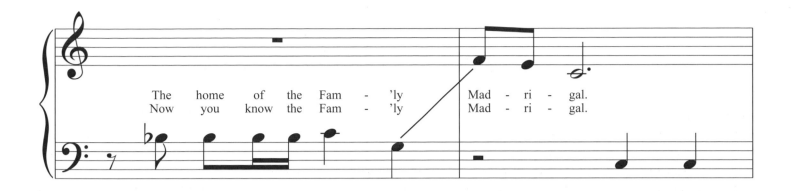

The home of the Fam - 'ly   Mad - ri - gal.
Now you know the Fam - 'ly   Mad - ri - gal.

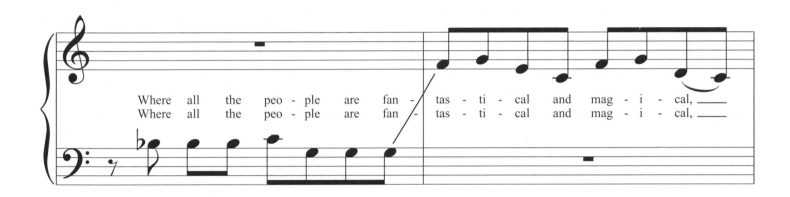

Where all the peo - ple are fan - tas - ti - cal and mag - i - cal, ____
Where all the peo - ple are fan - tas - ti - cal and mag - i - cal, ____

1.

I'm part of the Fam - 'ly   Mad - ri - gal!

2.

that's who we are in the Fam - 'ly   Mad - ri - gal!   *¡Adios!*

WAITING ON A MIRACLE

Music and Lyrics by
LIN-MANUEL MIRANDA

Moderately slow, in 2

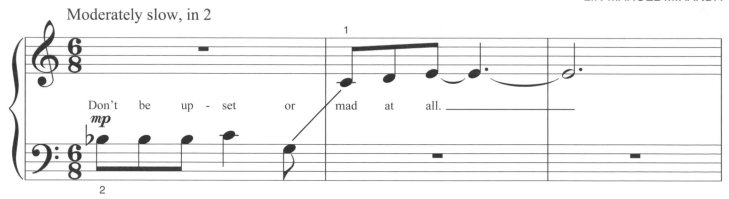

Don't be up-set or mad at all. _____

Don't feel re-gret, or sad at all. _____ Hey, I'm

still part of the Fam-'ly Mad-ri-gal _____ and I'm fine, I am to-tal-ly

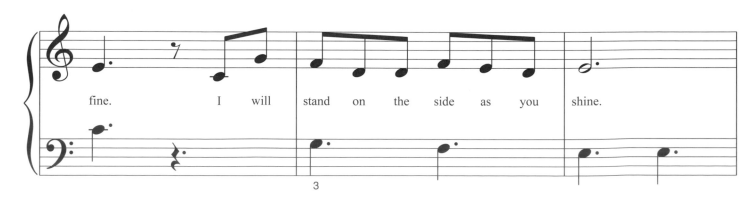

fine. I will stand on the side as you shine.

I'm not fine, I'm not fine...

I can't move ___ the moun - tains. ___ I can't make ___ the
I can't heal ___ what's bro - ken, ___ I can't con - trol ___ the

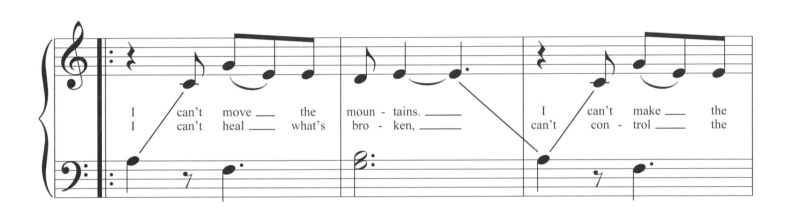

flow - ers bloom. I can't take ___ an - oth - er night up in my
morn - ing rain, I can't keep down the un - spo - ken in - vis - i - ble

room, wait - ing on a mir - a - cle. ___
pain, wait - ing on a mir - a - cle. ___

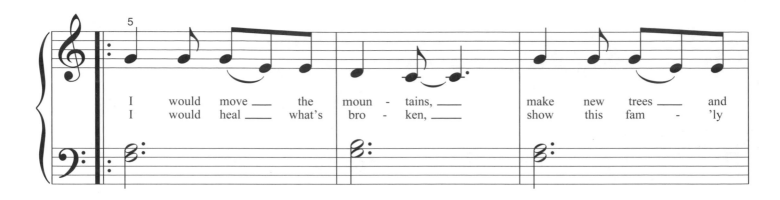

I would move ___ the moun - tains, ___ make new trees ___ and
I would heal ___ what's bro - ken, ___ show this fam - 'ly

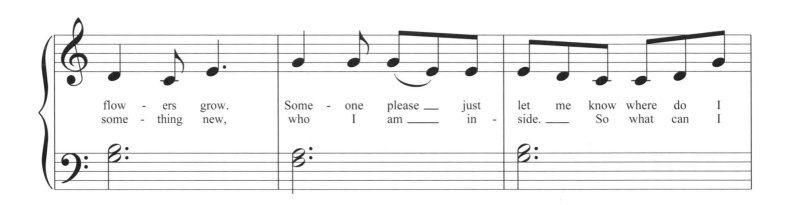

flow - ers grow. Some - one please ___ just let me know where do I
some - thing new, who I am ___ in - side. ___ So what can I

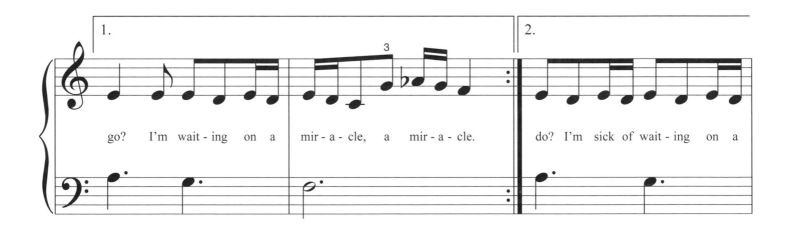

1.
go? I'm wait - ing on a mir - a - cle, a mir - a - cle.

2.
do? I'm sick of wait - ing on a

Slowly, freely

mir - a - cle, so here I go... Am I too late for a mir - a - cle? ___

WE DON'T TALK ABOUT BRUNO

Music and Lyrics by
LIN-MANUEL MIRANDA

Moderately

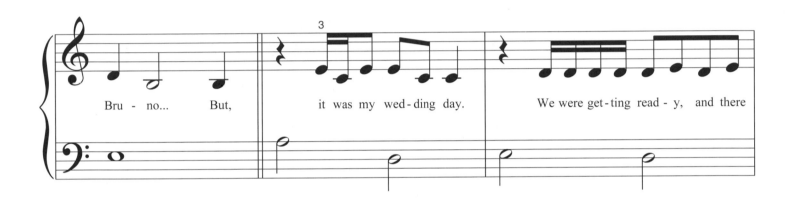

Bru - no says, "It looks like rain." In do - ing so, he floods my

brain. Mar - ried in a hur - ri - cane...

We don't talk a - bout Bru - no, no, no, no! We don't talk a - bout Bru-

- no! A sev - en - foot frame, rats a - long his back. When he

calls your name it all fades to black. Yeah, he sees your dreams and

feasts on your screams. We don't talk a-bout Bru - no, no, _____ no, no! _____

_____ We don't talk a-bout Bru - no! _____ _____ Don't talk a-bout Bru -

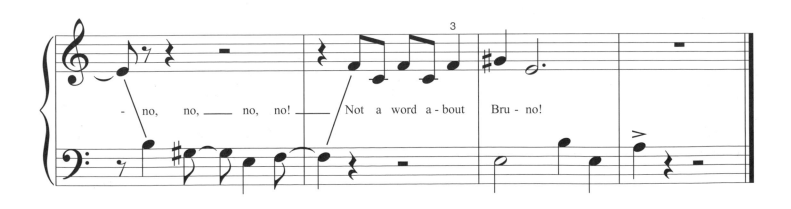

- no, no, _____ no, no! _____ Not a word a-bout Bru - no!

SURFACE PRESSURE

Music and Lyrics by
LIN-MANUEL MIRANDA

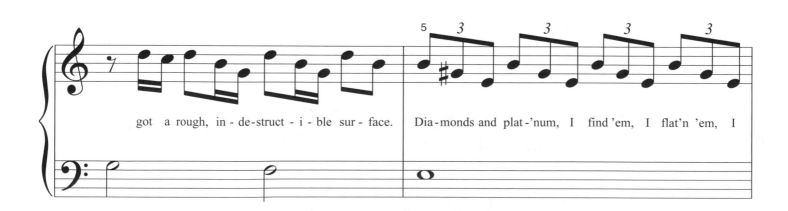

take what I'm hand - ed, I break what's de - mand - ed, but...

Un - der the sur - face, I feel ber-serk as a tight - rope walk - er in a three - ring cir - cus.

Un - der the sur - face, was Her - cu - les ev - er like, "Yo, I don't wan - na fight Cer - berus?"

Un - der the sur - face, I'm pret - ty sure I'm worth-less if I can't be of ser - vice, A

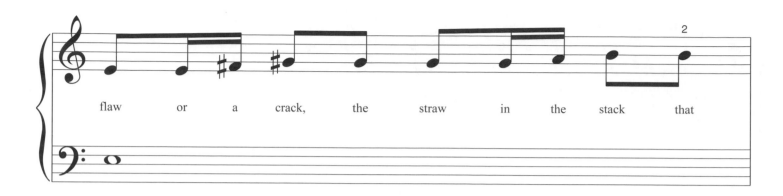

flaw or a crack, the straw in the stack that

breaks the cam - el's back. What breaks the cam - el's back? It's

pres - sure like a drip, drip, drip that - 'll nev - er stop, whoa, __

Pres - sure like a grip, grip, grip and it won't let go, whoa. __

Pres - sure that - 'll tip, tip, tip 'til you just go pop, whoa __ oh oh.

Pres - sure like a tick, tick, tick 'til it's ready to blow, whoa __ oh oh.

Give it to your sis - ter, your sis - ter's old - er.
Give it to your sis - ter, your sis - ter's strong - er.

Give her all the heav - y things we can't shoul - der.
See if she can hang on a lit - tle long - er.

Who am I if I can't run with the ball? _____ If I fall to...
Who am I if I don't have what it

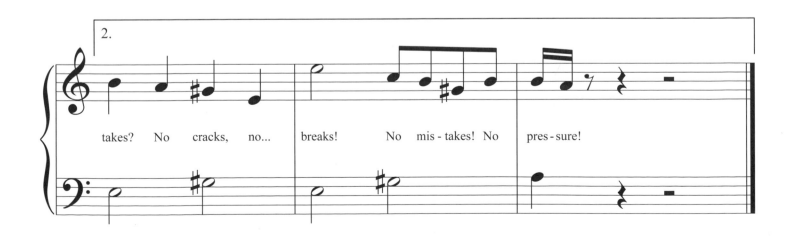

takes? No cracks, no... breaks! No mis - takes! No pres - sure!

ALL OF YOU

Music and Lyrics by
LIN-MANUEL MIRANDA

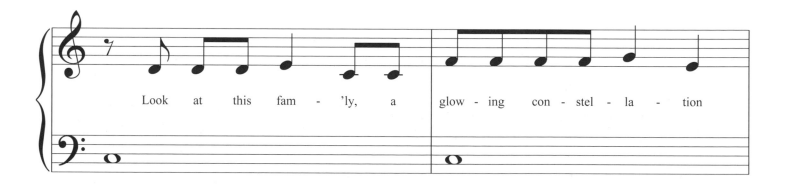

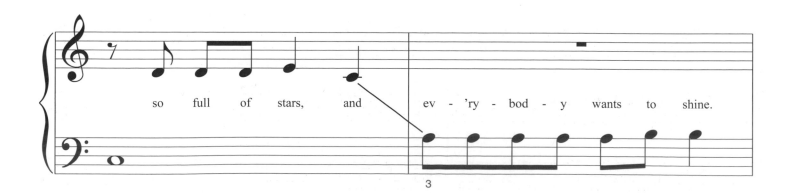

But the stars don't shine, they burn, and the

con - stel - la - tions shift. I think it's time you

learn: ____ You're more than just your gift. And I'm sor - ry I held

on too tight, just so a - fraid I'd lose you, too.

The mir - a - cle is not some mag - ic that you've

got. The mir - a - cle is you. Not some gift, just

you... The mir - a - cle is you. All of you, ___ all of you. ___

All of you, ___ all of you. ___

WHAT ELSE CAN I DO?

Music and Lyrics by
LIN-MANUEL MIRANDA

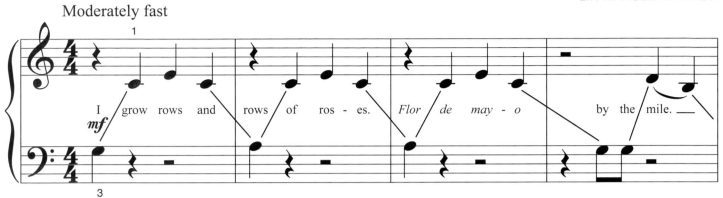

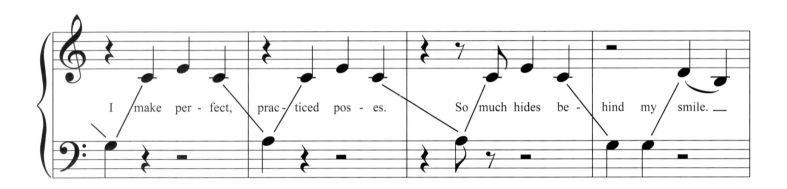

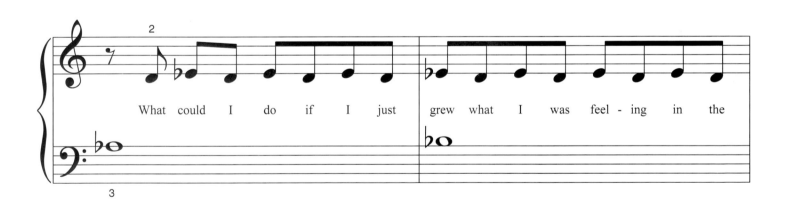

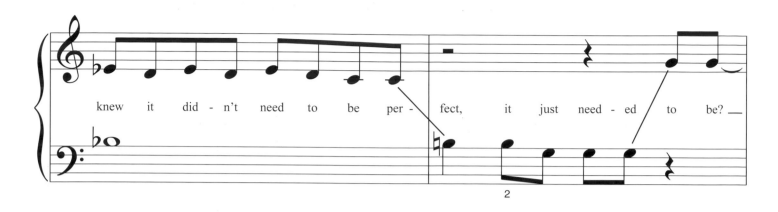

knew it did - n't need to be per - fect, it just need - ed to be? ___

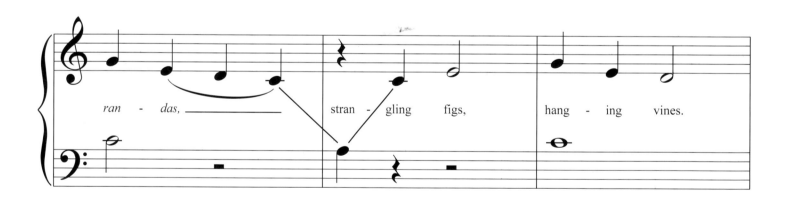

___ And they let me be? A hur - ri - cane of ja - ca -

ran - das, _____ stran - gling figs, hang - ing vines.

Pal - ma de ce - ra fills the air as I _____ climb and I push

To Coda ⊕

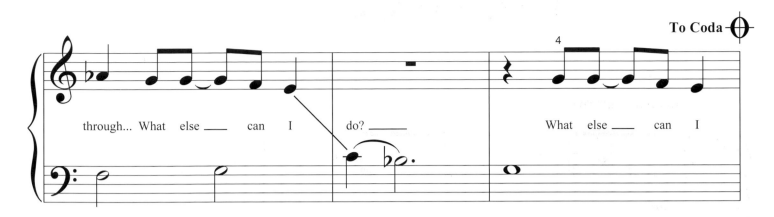

through... What else ___ can I do? ___

What else ___ can I

do?
All I know are the blos-soms you grow, but it's awe-some to see how you

D.S. al Coda

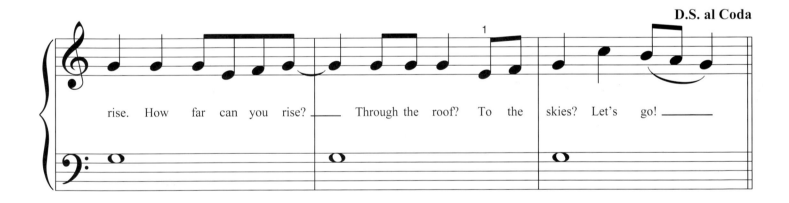

rise. How far can you rise? ___ Through the roof? To the skies? Let's go! ___

CODA
⊕

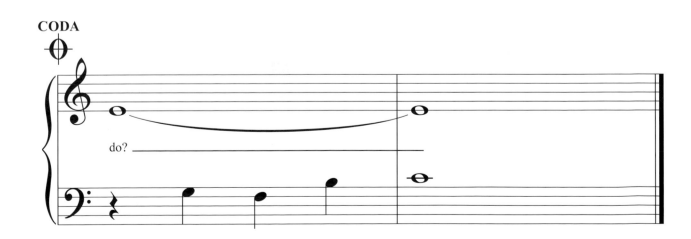

do? ___

DOS ORUGUITAS

Music and Lyrics by
LIN-MANUEL MIRANDA

Syncopated groove

Dos or - u - gui - tas,
Dos or - u - gui - tas

e - na - mo - ra - das,
pa - ran el vien - to,
pa - san sus no - ches
mien - tras se a - bra - zan
y ma - dru - ga - das.
con sen - ti - mien - to.

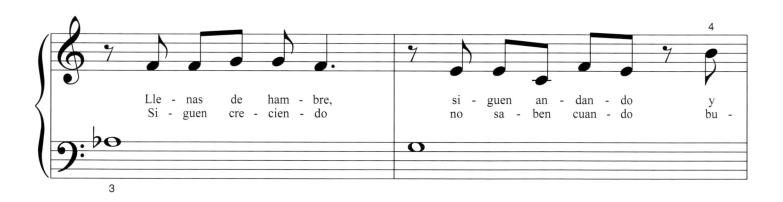

Lle - nas de ham - bre,
Si - guen cre - cien - do
si - guen an - dan - do
no sa - ben cuan - do
y
bu -

na - ve - gan - do un mun - do
scar al - gun rin - cón.
que
El
cam - bia y si - gue cam - bian - do
tiem - po si - gue cam - bian - do.
In

na - ve - gan - do un mun - do que cam - bia y si - gue cam - bian - do.
se - pa - ra - bles son y el tiem - po si - gue cam - bian - do.

Ay, or - u - gui - tas, no se a - guan - ten más. Hay ___ que cre - cer a - part - te y vol - ver,

ha - cia a - de - lan - te se gui - rás. Vie - nen mi - la - gros, vie - nen cri - sá - li - das.

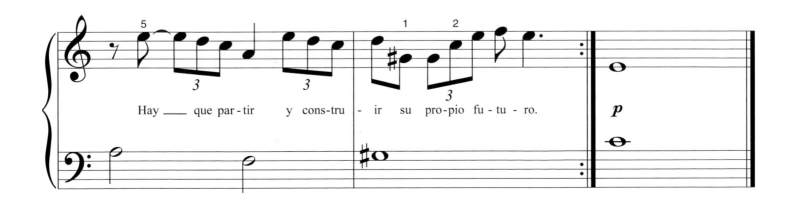

Hay ___ que par - tir y cons - tru - ir su pro - pio fu - tu - ro. *p*

COLOMBIA, MI ENCANTO

Music and Lyrics by
LIN-MANUEL MIRANDA

Moderately fast

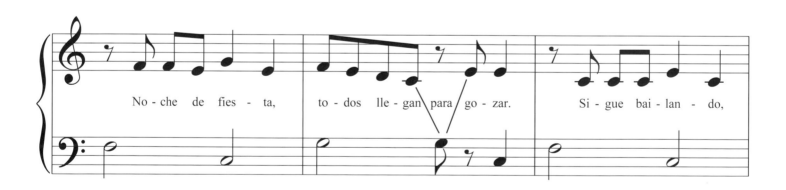

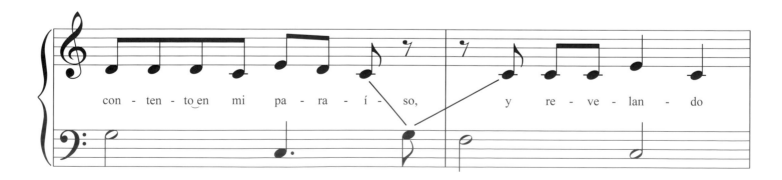

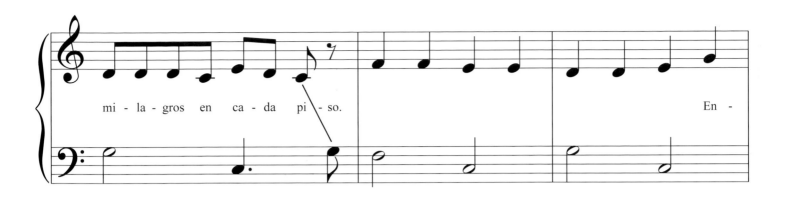

tan - to. _____ Te si - gue ben - di - cien - do tu en -

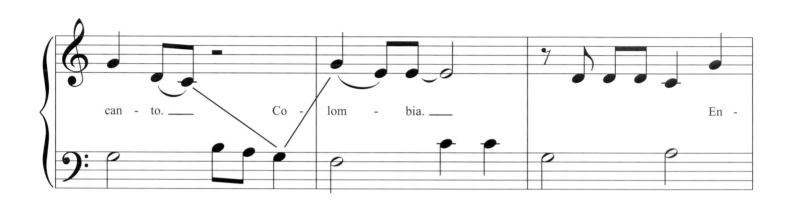

can - to. _____ Co - lom - bia. _____ En -

can - to. En - can - to.

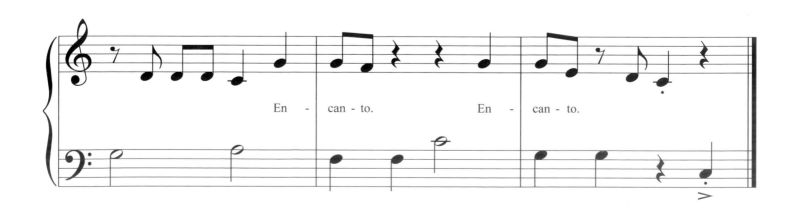

En - can - to. En - can - to.